FIND I✝HERE

FIND IT HERE

Dan F. Bienek

TATE PUBLISHING
AND ENTERPRISES, LLC

Published by Tate Publishing & Enterprises, LLC
127 E. Trade Center Terrace | Mustang, Oklahoma 73064 USA
1.888.361.9473 | www.tatepublishing.com

Tate Publishing is committed to excellence in the publishing industry. The company reflects the philosophy established by the founders, based on Psalm 68:11,
"The Lord gave the word and great was the company of those who published it."

Book design copyright © 2014 by Tate Publishing, LLC. All rights reserved.
Cover design by Allen Jomoc
Interior design by Joana Quilantang

Published in the United States of America

ISBN: 978-1-62994-065-6
Religion / Biblical Reference / General
14.03.07

PREFACE

The HOLY BIBLE used to create this recapitulation
Containing the Old and New Testaments
-OF-
The King James Version
Translated from the original tongues:
And with the former translations
Diligently compared and revised,
By His Majesty's special command

INTRODUCTION

WHAT DOES THE BIBLE SAY REGARDING:

Marriage-Divorce-The Ten Commandments-How to live your life-Tattos-Adultery-The House of the Lord God-Jesus-The end of the earth-The twelve Disciples-Lawyers-Forgivable sins and unforgivable sins-Joy in heaven-Eternal life-Judgment-Salvation for the Gentiles-Lesbians/Gays-Baptism-How to be saved-Love-The Ressurrection-Judgement-Forgiveness of sins-The purpose and the reason-Money-The evil tongue-Do not judge others-God's mercy and promise-Who is God-The Devil's number-Eternal hell-The end of Sata/Devil-Judgement with the book of Life-New Heaven and New Earth-God is coming.

LISTED INSIDE FOR A QUICK REFERENCE IS GOD'S WORD AND THE EXACT BOOK, CHAPTER AND VERSE(S) ANSWERING THESE QUESTIONS AND MUCH MORE

INDEX

CONTENTS

THE OLD TESTAMENT

The Beginning: Genesis 1, Verse 1

In the beginning God created the heaven and the earth.

God created Man & Woman: Genesis 1, verses 26-28

(26) And God said, Let us make man in our image, after our likeness: and let them have dominion over the fish of the sea, and over the fowl of the air, and over the cattle, and over all the earth, and over every creeping thing that creepeth upon the earth. (27) So God created man in his own image, in the image of God created he him; male and female created he them. (28) And God blessed them, and God said to unto them, Be fruitful, and multiply, and replenish the earth, and subdue it: and have dominion over the fish of the sea, and over the fowl of the air, and over every living thing that moveth upon the earth.

God created Man & Woman: Genesis 2, verses 4-7 & 18, & 21-24

(4) These are the generations of the heavens and of the earth when they were created, in the day that the Lord God made the earth and the heavens, (5)and every plant of the field before it was in the earth, and every herb of the field before it grew; for the Lord God had not caused it to rain upon the earth, and there was not a man to till the ground. (6) but there went up a mist from the earth, and watered the whole face of the ground (7) And the Lord God formed man of the dust of the ground, and breathed into his nostrils the breath of life; and man became a living soul. (18) And the Lord God said, It is not good that the man should be alone; I will make him an help meet for him." (21) And the Lord God caused a deep sleep to fall upon Adam, and he slept; and he took one of his ribs, and closed up the flesh instead thereof; (22) and the rib, which the Lord God had taken from the man, made he a woman, and brought her unto the man. (23) And Adam said, This is now bone of my bones, and flesh of my flesh; she shall be called Woman, because she was taken out of Man. (24) Therefore shall a man leave his father and his mother, and shall cleave unto his wife; and they shall be one flesh. (25) And they were both naked, the man and his wife, and were not ashamed.

The Garden of Eden and Sin: Genesis 2, verses 8-9

(8) And the Lord God planted a garden eastward in Eden; and there he put the man whom he had formed. (9) And out of the ground made the Lord God to grow every tree that is pleasant to the sight, and good for food; the tree of life also in the midst of the garden, and the tree of the knowledge of good and evil.

The Garden of Eden and sin: Genesis 3, verses 1-24

Now the serpent was more subtle than any beast of the field which the Lord God had made. And he said unto the woman, Yea, hath God said, Ye shall not eat of every tree of the garden? (2) And the woman said unto the serpent, We may eat of the fruit of the trees of the garden; (3) But of the fruit of the tree which is in the midst of the garden, God hath said, Ye shall not eat of it, neither shall you touch it, lest ye die. (4) And the serpent said unto the woman, Ye shall not surely die; (5) For God doth know that in the day, ye eat thereof, then your eyes shall be opened, and ye shall be as Gods, knowing good and evil. (6) and when the woman saw that the tree was good for food, and that it was pleasant to the eyes, and a tree to be desired to make one wise, she took of the fruit thereof and did eat, and gave also unto her husband with her; and he did eat. (7) And the eyes of them both were opened, and they knew that they were naked; and they sewed fig leaves together, and made themselves aprons. (8) And they heard the voice of the Lord God walking in the garden in the cool of the day; and Adam and his wife hid themselves from the presence of the Lord God amongest the trees of the garden. (9) And the Lord God called unto Adam, and said unto him, Where art thou? (10) And he said, I heard thy voce in the garden, and I was afraid, because I was naked; and I hid myself." (11) And he said, Who told thee that thou wast naked? Hast thou eaten of the tree, whereof I commanded thee that thou shouldest not eat?" (12) And the man said, The woman whom thou gavest to be with me, she gave me of the tree, and I did eat. (13) And the Lord God said unto the woman, What is this that thou hast done? And the woman said, "The serpent beguiled me, and I did eat. (14) And the Lord God said unto the serpent, Because thou hast done this, thou art cursed above all cattle, and above every beast of the field; upon thy belly shalt thou go, and dust shall thou eat all the days of thy life. (15) I will put enmity between thee and the woman, and between thy seed and her seed; it shall bruise thy head, and thou shall bruise his heel." (16) Unto the woman he said, I will greatly multiply thy sorrow and thy conception; in sorrow thou shall bring forth children, and thy desire shall be to thy husband, and he shall rule over thee. (17) And unto Adam he said, "Because thou hast hearkened unto the voice of thy wife, and hast eaten of the tree, of which I commanded thee, saying thou shall not eat of it; cursed is the ground for thy sake; in sorrow shalt thou eat of it all the days of thy life;

(18) Thorns also and thistles shall it bring forth to thee; and thou shalt eat the herb of the field; (19) In the sweat of thy face shalt thou eat bread, till thou return unto the ground; for out of it wast thou taken; for dust thou art, and unto dust shalt thou return. (20) And Adam called his wife's name Eve; because she was the mother of all living. (21) Unto Adam also and to his wife did the Lord God make coats of skins, and clothed them. (22) And the Lord God said, Behold, the man has become as one of us, to know good and evil; and now, lest he put forth his hand and take also of the tree of life, and eat, and live for ever–(23) Therefore the Lord God sent him forth from the garden of Eden, to till the ground from whence he was taken. (24) So he drove out the man; and he placed at the east of the Garden of Eden Cherubims, and a flaming sword which turned every way, to keep the way of the tree of life.

Adam lived to be 930 years old (Genesis 5, verse 5)

"Noah was 600 years old when the flood of waters came unto the earth

- The flood was for forty days and forty nights
- The water covered the whole earth and the mountains. The water was fifteen cubits deep above the mountain tops.
- The waters receded daily and finally after 150 days the ARK came to rest upon the mountains of Ararat on July 17 and the waters continued to abate until the tenth month;

Dan F. Bienek

- "Noah lived to be 950 years old (Genesis 9, verse 29)

- The covenant between Abraham and God was that all males shall be circumcised. (Genesis 17, verse 11) at eight days old. Abraham was ninety-nine years old when he was circumcised

- Moses died at the age of 120 (Deuteronomy 34, verse 7)

The Ten Commandments: Exodus 20, Verses 2-17

(2) I am the Lord thy God, which have brought thee out of the land of Egypt, out of the house of bondage.

(3) Thou shalt have no other gods before me. (4) Thou shalt not make unto thee any graven image, or any likeness of anything that is in heaven above, or that is in the earth beneath, or that is in the water under the earth; (5) Thou shalt not bow down thyself to them or serve them; for I the Lord thy God am a jealous God, visiting the iniquity of the fathers upon the children unto the third and fourth generation of them that hate me; (6) And shewing mercy unto thousands of them that love me, and keep my commandments.

(7) Thou shalt not take the name of the Lord thy God in vain; for the Lord will not hold him guiltless that taketh his name in vain.

(8) Remember the Sabbath day, to keep it holy. (9) Six days shalt thou labour, and do all thy work; (10)

But the seventh day is the Sabbath of the Lord thy God; in it thou shalt not do any work, thou, nor thy son, nor thy daughter, thy manservant, nor thy maidservant, nor thy cattle, nor thy stranger that is within thy gates; (11) For in six days the Lord made heaven and earth, the sea, and all that in them is, and rested the seventh day; wherefore the Lord blessed the Sabbath day, and hallowed it.

(12) Honor thy father and thy mother, that thy days may be long upon the land which the Lord thy God giveth thee.

(13) Thou shalt not kill.

(14) Thou shalt not commit adultery.

(15) Thou shalt not steal.

(16) Thou shalt not bear false witness against thy neighbour.

(17) Thou shalt not covet your neighbour's house; thou shalt not covet thy neighbour's wife, nor his manservant, nor his maidservant, nor his ox, nor his ass, nor anything that is thy neighbour's.

The Ten Commandments: Deuteronomy 5, Verses 6-21

(6) I am the Lord thy God, which brought thee out of the land of Egypt, from the house of bondage.

(7) Thou shalt have none other gods before me. (8) Thou shalt not make thee any graven image, or any likeness of anything that is in heaven above, or that is in the earth beneath, or that is in the waters

beneath the earth; (9) Thou shalt not bow down thyself unto them nor serve them; for I the Lord thy God am a jealous God, visiting the iniquity of the fathers upon the children unto the third and fourth generation of them that hate me; (10) And showing mercy unto thousands of them that love me and keep my commandments.

(11) Thou shalt not take the name of the Lord thy God in vain; for the Lord will not hold him guiltless that taketh his name in vain.

(12) Keep the Sabbath day, to sanctify it, as the Lord thy God hath commanded thee. (13) Six days thou shalt labour, and do all thy work; (14) But the seventh day is the Sabbath of the Lord thy God; in it thou shalt not do any work, thou, nor thy son, nor thy daughter, nor thy manservant, nor thy maidservant, nor thine ox, nor thine ass, nor any of thy cattle, nor thy stranger that is within thy gates; that thy manservant and thy maidservant may rest as well as thou. (15) And remember that thou wast a servant in the land of Egypt, and that the Lord thy God brought thee out thence through a mighty hand and by a stretched out arm; therefore the Lord thy God commanded thee to keep the Sabbath day.

(16) Honor thy father and thy mother, as the Lord thy God hath commanded thee; That thy days may be prolonged, and that it may go well with thee, in the land which the Lord thy God giveth thee.

(17) Thou shalt not kill.

(18) Neither shalt thou commit adultery.

(19) Neither shalt thou steal.

(20) Neither shalt thou bear false witness against thy neighbour.

(21) Neither shalt thou desire thy neighbour's wife, neither shalt thou covet thy neighbour's house; his field, or his manservant, or his maidservant, his ox, or his ass, or anything that is thy neighbour's."

How to live your life: Exodus 21, verses 1-31

Now these are the ordinances which you shall set before them.

(Highlights): Some of the many ordinances written

(12) He that smiteth a man, so that he die, shall be surely put to death.

(15) And he that smiteth his father, or his mother, shall be surely put to death.

(16) And he that stealeth a man, and selleth him, or if he be found in his hand, he shall surely be put to death.

(17) And he that curseth his father, or his mother, shall surely be put to death.

(18) And if men strive together, and one smite another with a stone, or with his fist, and he die not but keepeth his bed; (19) if he rise again, and walk abroad upon his staff, then shall he that smote him be quit; only he shall pay for the loss of his time, and shall cause him to be thoroughly healed.

(22) If men strive, and hurt a woman with child, so that her fruit depart from her, and yet no mischief follow; he shall be surely punished, according as the woman's husband will lay upon him, and he shall pay as the judges determine. (23) And If any mischief follow, then thou shalt give life for life, (24) eye for eye, tooth for tooth, hand for hand, foot for foot, (25) burning for burning, wound for wound, stripe for stripe.

Eye for an Eye: Leviticus 24, Verse 17 & Verses 19-21

(17) And he that killeth any man shall surely be put to death. (19) And if a man cause a blemish in his neighbor; as he hath done, so shall it be done to him; (20) Breach for breach, eye for eye, tooth for tooth; as he hath caused a blemish in a man, so shall it be done to him again. (21) And he that killeth a beast, he shall restore it; and he that killeth a man, he shall be put to death. (22) Ye shall have one manner of law, as well for the stranger, as for one of your own country, for I am the Lord your God."

Not one witness shall prevail to convict: Deuteronomy 19, Verses 15-21

(15) One witness shall not rise up against a man for any iniquity, or for any sin, in any sin that he sinneth: at the mouth of two witnesses, or at the mouth of three witnesses, shall the matter be established. (16) If a false witness rise up against any man to testify against him that which is wrong, (17) Then both the men, between whom the controversy is, shall stand

before the Lord, before the priests and the judges, which shall be in those days; (18) And the judges shall make diligent inquisition: and behold if the witness be a false witness, and hath testified falsely against his brother; (19) Then shall ye do unto him, as he had thought to have done unto his brother; so shalt thou put the evil away from among you. (20) And those which remain shall hear, and fear, and shall henceforth commit no more any such evil among you. (21) And thine eye shall not pity: but life shall go for life, eye for eye, tooth for tooth, hand for hand, foot for foot.

Thou shall not work on the Sabbath (7th) day: Exodus 31, Verses 14-17

(14) Ye shall keep the Sabbath therefore; for it is holy unto you; everyone that defileth it shall surely be put to death; for whosoever doeth any work theirin, that soul shall be cut off from among his people. (15) Six days may work be done, but in the seventh day is the Sabbath of rest, holy to the Lord; whoever doeth any work in the Sabbath day, he shall surely be put to death. (16) Wherefore the children of Israel shall keep the Sabbath, to observe the Sabbath throughout their generations, for a perpetual covenant. (17) It is a sign between me and the children of Israel for ever, for in six days the Lord made heaven and earth, and on the seventh day he rested, and was refreshed.

Thou shall not work on the Sabbath (7th) day: Exodus 34, Verse 21

(21) Six days thou shalt work, but on the seventh day thou shalt rest; in earing time and in harvest thou shalt rest.

Thou shall not work on the Sabbath (7th) day: Exodus 35, Verses 2&3

(2) Six days shall work be done, but on the seventh day there shall be to you an holy day, a sabbath of rest to the Lord; whosoever doeth work therein shall be put to death.

The Ten Commandments of stone: Exodus 31, Verse 18

(18) And he gave unto Moses, when he had made an end of communing with him upon Mount Sinai, two tables of testimony, tables of stone, written with the finger of God.

No one is to see the face of God: Exodus 33, Verses 20-23

(20) And he said, Thou canst not see my face; for their shall no man see me, and live. (21) And the Lord said, Behold, there is a place by me, and thou shalt stand upon a rock; (22) And it shall come to pass, while my glory passes by, that I will put thee in a clift of the rock, and will cover thee with my hand while I pass by; (23) And I will take away mine hand, and thou shalt see my back parts; but my face shall not be seen."

God is: Exodus 34, Verses 6-8

(6) And the Lord passed by before him, and proclaimed, The Lord, The Lord God merciful and gracious, longsuffering, and abundant in goodness and truth, (7) Keeping mercy for thousands, forgiving iniquity and transgression and sin, and that will by no means clear the guilty; visiting the iniquity of the fathers upon the children and upon the children's children, unto the third and to the fourth generation. (8) And Moses made hast and bowed his head toward the earth, and worshipped.

How to Harvest: Leviticus 19, Verses 9&10

(9) And when ye reap the harvest of your land, thou shalt not wholly reap the corners of thy field, neither shalt thou gather the gleanings of thy harvest. (10) And thou shalt not glean thy vineyard , neither shalt thou gather every grape of thy vineyard; Thou shall leave them for the poor and stranger; I am the Lord your God.

How to Harvest: Leviticus 23, Verse 22

(22) And when ye reap the harvest of your land, thou shalt not make clean riddance of the corners of thy field when thou reapest, neither shalt thou gather any gleaning of thy harvest; Thou shall leave them unto the poor, and to the stranger: I am the Lord your God.

No tattoo's, no shaving: Leviticus 19, Verses 27 & 28

(27) Ye shall not round the corners of your heads, neither shalt thou mar the corners of thy beard. (28)

Ye shall not make any cuttings in your flesh for the dead, nor print any marks upon you: I am the Lord.

Wearing each other's clothes: Deuteronomy 22, Verse 5

(5) The woman shall not wear that which pertaineth unto a man, neither shall a man put on a woman's garment; for all that do so are abomination unto the Lord thy God.

Lying with the same sex or beast: Leviticus 18, Verses 22 & 23

(22) Thou shalt not lie with mankind, as with womankind: it is abomination. (23) Neither shalt thou lie with any beast to defile thyself therewith; neither shall any woman stand before a beast to lie down thereto: it is confusion.

Adultery, Incest and same sex: Leviticus 20, Verses 10-16

(10) And the man that committeth adultery with another man's wife, even he that committeth adultery with his neighbor's wife, the adulterer and the adulteress shall surely be put to death. (11) And the man that lieth with his father's wife hath uncovered his father's nakedness; both of them shall surely be put to death, their blood shall be upon them. (12) And if a man lie with his daughter in law, both of them shall surely be put to death; they have wrought confusion; their blood shall be upon them. (13) If a man also lie with mankind as he lieth with a woman, both of them have committed an abomina-

tion; they shall surely be put to death; their blood shall be upon them. (14) And if a man take a wife and her mother, it is wickedness; they shall be burnt with fire, both he and they; that there be no wickedness among you. (15) And if a man lie with a beast, he shall surely be put to death; and you shall slay the beast. (16) And if a woman approach unto any beast and lie down thereto, thou shalt kill the woman and the beast; they shall surely be put to death, their blood shall be upon them.

A priest marries a virgin only: Leviticus 21, Verses 13-15

(13) And he shall take a wife in her virginity. (14) A widow, or a divorced woman, or profane, or an harlot, these shall he not take; but he shall take a virgin of his own people to wife.

God's blessings to the people of Israel: Numbers 6, Verses 22-26

(22) And the Lord spake unto Moses, saying (23) "Speak unto Aaron and unto his sons, saying, On this wise ye shall bless the children of Israel, saying unto them, (24) The Lord bless thee and keep thee: (25) The Lord make his face shine upon thee, and be gracious unto thee: (26) The Lord lift up his countenance upon thee, and give thee peace.

The number of people who made it to Israel: Numbers 26, Verse 51

> (51) These were the numbered of the children of Israel, six hundred thousand and a thousand seven hundred and thirty (601,730)

The chosen people of Israel: Deuteronomy 7, Verses 6, 13, 14

> (6) For thou art an holy people unto the Lord thy God; the Lord thy God hath chosen thee to be a special people unto himself, above all people that are upon the face of the earth. (13) And he will love thee, bless thee, and multiply thee; he will also bless the fruit of thy womb, and the fruit of thy land, thy corn, and thy wine and thine oil, the increase of thy kine, and the flocks of thy sheep, in the land which he sware unto thy fathers to give thee. (14) Thou shall be blessed above all people; there shall not be male or female barren among you, or among your cattle.

The new 10 commandments of stone and the wooden ark: Deuteronomy 10, Verses 1-5

> (1) At that time the Lord said unto me, Hew thee two tables of stone like unto the first, and come up unto me into the mount, and make thee an ark of wood. (2) And I will write on the tables the words that were in the first tables which thou brakest, and thou shalt put them in the ark. (3) And I made an ark of shittim wood, and hewed two tables of stone like unto the first, and went up into the mount with the two tables in mine hand. (4) And

he wrote on the tables, according to the first writing, the ten commandments which the Lord spake unto you in the mount out of the midst of the fire in the day of the assembly; and the Lord gave them unto me. (5) And I turned myself and came down from the mount, and put the tables in the ark which I had made; and there they be, as the Lord commanded me.

The Ark of the Covenant: Joshua 3, Verses 14-17

(14) And it came to pass, when the people removed from their tents, to pass over Jordan, and the priests bearing the ark of the covenant before the people, (15) And as they that bare the ark where come unto Jordan, and the feet of the priests that bare the ark were dipped in the brim of the water (for Jordan overfloweth all his banks all the time of harvest), (16) That the waters which came down from above stood and rose up upon an heap very far from the city Adam,that is beside Zaretan; and those that came down toward the sea of the plain, even the salt sea, failed, and were cut off; and the people passed over right against Jericho. (17) And the priests that bare the ark of the covenant of the Lord , stood firm on dry ground in the midst of Jordan, and all thee Isralites passed over on dry ground, until all the people were passed clean over Jordan.

The release of debt among you: Deuteronomy 15, Verses 1-6

(1) At the end of every seven years thou shalt make a release. (2) And this is the manner of the release:

Every creditor that lendeth ought unto his neighbor shall release it; he shall not exact it of his neighbor, or of his brother, because it is called the Lord's release. (3) Of a foreigner thou mayest exact it again; but that which is thine with thy brother thine hand shall release. (4) Save when there shall be no poor among you ; for the Lord shall greatly bless thee in the land which the Lord thy God giveth thee for an inheritance to possess it; (5) Only if thou carefully hearken unto the voice of the Lord thy God, to observe to do all these commandments which I command thee this day. (6) For the Lord thy God blesseth thee, as he promised thee, and thou shalt lend unto many nations, but thou shalt not borrow; and thou shalt reign over many nations, but they shall not reign over thee.

No bastard shall enter church: Deuteronomy 23, Verses 1 & 2

(1) He that is wounded in the stones, or hath his privy member cut off, shall not enter into the congregation of the Lord. (2) A bastard shall not enter into the congregation of the Lord; even to the tenth generation shall he not enter into the congregation of the Lord.

Joshua replaces Moses: Joshua 1, Verses 1-3

(1) Now after the death of Moses the servant of the Lord it came to pass, that the Lord spake unto Joshua the son of Nun, Moses 'minister, saying, (2) Moses my servant is dead; now therefore arise, go

over this Jordan, thou, and all this people, unto the land which I do give to them, even to the children of Israel. (3) Every place that the sole of your foot shall tread upon, that have I given unto you, as I said unto Moses.

Samson: Judges 13, Verse 24

(24) And the woman bare a son, and called his name Samson; and the child grew, and the Lord blessed him.

Samson was the son of Mano'ah

Samson's hair was his strength

He was a Nazirite to God from the time of his birth

The Ark of the Covenant was stolen by the Philistines: 1Samuel 4, Verses 10-11

(10) And the Philistines fought, and Israel was smitten, and they fled, every man into his tent; and there was a very great slaughter; for there fell of Israel thirty thousand footmen. (11) And the ark of God was taken; and the two sons of Eli, Hophni and Phinehas, were slain.

The Ark of the Lord was in the Philistines cities of Ashdod, Garth and Ekron: 1Samuel 5, Verse 1-4–Verses 6-12

(1) And the Philistines took the ark of God, and brought it from Ebenezer unto Ashdod; (2) When the Philistines took the ark of God, they brought it into the house of Dagon and set it by Dagon. (3)

And when they of Ashdod arose early on the morrow, behold, Dagon was fallen upon his face to the earth before the Ark of the Lord. And they took Dagon and set him in his place again. (4) And when they arose early on the morrow morning, behold, Dagon was fallen upon his face to the ground before the ark of the Lord; and the head of Dagon and both the palms of his hands were cut off upon the threshold; only the stump of Dagon was left to him.

(6) But the hand of the Lord was heavy upon them of Ashdod, and he destroyed them, and smote them with emerods, even Ashdod and the coasts thereof. (7) And when the men of Ashdod saw that it was so, they said, The Ark of the God of Israel shall not abide with us: for his hand is sore upon us and upon Dagon our God. (8) They sent therefore and gathered all the lords of the Philistines unto them, and said, What shall we do with the ark of the God of Israel? And they answered, Let the ark of the God of Israel be carried about unto Gath. And they carried the ark of the God of Israel about thither. (9) And it was so. That, after they had carried it about, the hand of the Lord was against the city with a very great destruction; and he smote the men of the city, both small and great, and they had emerods in their secret parts. (10) Therefore they sent the ark of God to Ekron. And it came to pass as the ark of God came to Ekron, that the Ekronites cried out, saying, They have brought about the ark of the God of Israel to us, to slay us and our people. (11) So they sent and gathered together all the lords of the

Philistines, and said, Send away the ark of the God of Israel, and let it go again to his own place, that it slay us not, and our people. for there was a deathly destruction throughout all the city; the hand of God was very heavy there; (12) And the men that died not were smitten with the emerods; and the cry of the city went up to heaven.

The Ark of the God of Israel was sent away in a cart drawn by two milch cows: 1Samuel 6, Verses 1-3

(1) And the Ark of the Lord was in the country of the Philistines seven months. (2) And the Philistines called for the priests and the diviners, saying, What shall we do to the ark of the Lord? tell us wherewith we shall send it to its place. (3) And they said, If ye send away the ark of the God of Israel, send it not empty; but in any wise return him a trespass offering; then ye shall be healed, and it shall be known to you why his hand is not removed from you.

The story of David and Goliath: 1 Samuel 17, Verses 4-15

(4) And there went out a champion out of the camp of the Philistines, named Goliath, of Gath, whose height was six cubits and a span. (5) And he had an helmet of brass upon his head, and he was armed with a coat of mail; and the weight of the coat was five thousand shekels of brass. (6) And he had greaves of brass upon his legs, and a target of brass between his shoulders. (7) And the staff of his spear was like a weaver's beam; and his spear's head

weighted six hundred shekels of iron; and one bearing a shield went before him. (8) And he stood and cried unto the armies of Israel, And said unto them, Why are ye come out to set your battle in aray? Am I not a Philistine, and ye servants to Saul? Choose you a man for you, and let him come down to me. (9) If he be able to fight with me and to kill me, then will we be your servants; but if I prevail against him, and kill him, then shall ye be our servants and serve us." (12) Now David was the son of an Ephrathite of Bethlehem-judah, whose name was Jesse, and he had eight sons: and the man went among men for an old man in the days of Saul. (13) And the three eldest sons of Jesse went and followed Saul to the battle: and the names of his three sons that went to the battle were Eliab the first born and next unto him Abinadab, and the third Shammah.(14) And David was the youngest; and the three eldest followed Saul, (15) But David went and returned from Saul to feed his father's sheep at Bethlehem. (32) And David said to Saul, Let no man's heart fail because of him; thy servant will go and fight with this Philistine. (37) David said, Moreover,The Lord that delivered me out of the paw of the lion, and out of the paw of the bear, will deliver me out of the hand of this Philistine. And Saul said unto David, Go, and the Lord be with thee. (40) And he took his staff in his hand, and chose him five smooth stones out of the brook, and put them in a shepherd's bag which he had, even in a scrip; and his sling was in his hand; and he drew near to the Philistine. (48)And it came to pass, when the Philistine arose; and came and drew nigh to meet David, that David hasted and ran toward the army to meet the Philistine. (49) And David put his hand in his bag, and took thence a stone, and slang it, and smote the Philistine in his forehead; that the stone sunk into his forehead, and he fell upon his face to the earth. (50) So David prevailed over the Philistine with a sling and with a stone, and smote the Philistine, and slew him; but there was no sword in the hand of David.

David became King of Israel: 2 Samuel 5, Verses 1-5

(1) Then came all the tribes of Israel to David unto Hebron, and spake, saying Behold, we are thy bone and thy flesh. (2) Also in time past, when Saul was king over us, thou wast he that leadest out and broughtest in Israel; and the Lord said to thee, Thou shalt feed my people Israel, and thou shalt be a captain over Israel. (3) So all the elders of Israel, came to the king to Hebron; and king David made a league with them in Hebron before the Lord; and they anointed David king over Israel. (4) David was thirty years old when he began to reign, and he reigned forty years. (5) In Hebron he reigned over Judah seven years and six months; and in Jerusalem he reigned thirty and three years over all Israel and Judah.

Elijah the Prophet–the only person to ascend into heaven without dying first: 2 Kings 2, Verses 1-12

(1) And it came to pass, when the Lord would take up Elijah into heaven by a whirlwind, that Elijah went with Elisha from Gilgal. (2) And Elijah said unto Elisha, Tarry here, I pray thee; for the Lord hath sent me to Bethel. And Elisha said unto him, As the Lord liveth, and as thy soul liveth, I will not leave thee. So they went down to Bethel. (3) And the sons of the prophets that were at Bethel came forth to Elisha, and said unto him, Knowest thou that the Lord will take away thy master from thy head to day?" And he said, Yea, I know it; hold ye your peace. (4) And Elijah said unto him, Elisha, tarry here, I pray thee; for the Lord hath sent me to Jericho. And he said, As the Lord liveth, and as thy soul liveth, I will not leave thee, So they came to Jericho. (5) And the sons of the prophets that were at Jericho came to Elisha, and said unto him, Knowest thou that the Lord will take away thy master from thy head today?" And he answered, yea I know it; hold ye your peace. (6) And Elijah said unto him, Tarry, I pray thee, here; for the Lord hath sent me to Jordan. And he said, As the Lord liveth, and as thy soul liveth, I will not leave thee. And they two went on. (7) And fifty men of the sons of the prophets, went, and stood to view afar off; and they two stood by Jordan. (8) And Elijah took his mantle, and wrapped it together, and smote the waters, and they were divided hither and thither, so that they two went over on dry ground. (9) And it came to pass when they were gone over, that Elijah said unto Elisha, Ask what I shall do for thee, before I be taken away from thee. And Elisha said, I pray thee,

let a double portion of thy spirit be upon me. (10) And he said, Thou hast asked a hard thing, nevertheless, if thou see me when I am taken from thee, it shall be so unto thee; but if not, it shall not be so." (11) And it came to pass, as they still went on, and talked, that, behold there appeared a chariot of fire, and horses of fire, and parted them both asunder; and Elijah went up by a whirlwind into heaven. (12) And Elisha saw it and he cried, My father, my father, the chariot of Israel, and the horsemen thereof. And he saw him no more; and he took hold of his own clothes, and rent them in two pieces.

The House of the Lord God: 2 Chronicles Chapter 3 Verses 1-7

(1) Then Solomon began to build the house of the Lord at Jerusalem in Mount Moriah, where the Lord appeared unto David his father, in the place that David had prepared in the threshing floor of Ornan the Jebusite. (2) And he began to build in the second day of the second month, in the fourth year of his reign. (3) Now these are the things wherein Solomon was instructed for the building of the house of God. The length by cubits after the first measure was threescore cubits, and the breadth twenty cubits. (4) And the porch that was in the front of the house, the length of it was according to the breadth of the house twenty cubits, and the height was an hundred and twenty: and he overlaid it within with pure gold. (5) And the greater house he ceiled with fir tree, which he overlaid with

fine gold, and set thereon palm trees and chains. (6) And he garnished the house with precious stones for beauty: and the gold was gold of Parvaim. (7) He overlaid also the house, the beams, the posts, and the walls thereof and the doors thereof, with gold; and graved cherubims on the walls.

King Solomon's dedication of the house of God: 2 Chronicles 6, Verses 3-11

(3) And the king turned his face, and blessed the whole congregation of Israel: and all the congregation of Israel stood. (4) And he said, Blessed be the Lord God of Israel, who hath with his hands fulfilled that which he spake with his mouth to my father David, saying, (5) Since the day that I brought forth my people out of the land of Egypt I chose no city among all the tribes of Israel to build an house in, that my name might be there; neither chose I any man to be a ruler over my people Israel; (6) But I have chosen Jerusalem, that my name might be there; and have chosen David to be over my people Israel. (7) Now it was in the heart of David my father to build an house for the name of the Lord God of Israel. (8) But the Lord said to David my father, Forasmuch as it was in thine heart to build an house for my name, thou didst well in that it was in thine heart; (9) Notwithstanding thou shalt not build the house; but thy son which shall come forth out of thy loins, he shall build the house for my name. (10) The Lord therefor hath performed his word that he hath spoken: for I am

risen up in the room of David my father, and am set on the throne of Israel, as the Lord promised, and have built the house for the name of the Lord God of Israel. (11) And in it have I put the ark, wherein is the covenant of the Lord, that he made with the children of Israel.

Rehoboam (the son of Solomon) had many wives and concubines: 2 Chronicles 11, verses 18-21

(18) And Rehoboam took him Mahalath the daughter of Jerimoth the son of David to wife, and Abihail the Daughter of Eliab the son of Jesse; (19) which bare him children; Jeush, and Shermariah and Zaham. (20) And after her he took Maacah the daughter of Absalom, which bare him Abijah, and Attai, and Ziza, and Shelomith. (21) And Rehoboam loved Maacah the daughter of Absalom above all his wives and concubines; (for he took eighteen wives, and three score concubines, and begat twenty and eight sons, and threescore daughters.)

Some of the *Special Quotes* from the Old Testament:

Psalms 19, Verse 14: (14) Let the words of my mouth, and the meditation of my heart, be acceptable in thy sight, O Lord, my strenght and my redeemer.

Psalms 23, Verses 1-6:

(1) The Lord is my shepherd, I shall not want; (2) He maketh me to lie down in green pastures. He leadeth me beside the still waters; (3) He restoreth my soul: he leadth me in paths of rightcousness for

his names' sake. (4) Yeah, though I walk through the valley of the shadow of death, I will fear no evil: for thou art with me; thy rod and thy staff they comfort me. (5) Thou preparest a table before me in the presence of mine enemies: thou anointest my head with oil; my cup runneth over. (6) Surely goodness and mercy shall follow me all the days of my life; and I will dwell in the house of the Lord for ever.

Psalms 32, Verse 1-2:

(1) Blessed is he whose transgression is forgiven, whose sin is covered. (2) Blessed is the man unto whom the Lord imputeth not iniquity, and in whose spirit there is no guile.

Psalms 41, Verse 4:

(4) I said, Lord, be merciful unto me; heal my soul; for I have sinned against thee.

Psalms 94, Verses 8-11:

(8) Understand, ye brutish among the people: And ye fools, when will ye be wise? (9) He that planted the ear, shall he not hear? He that formed the eye, shall he not see? (10) He that chastiseth the heathen, shall not he correct? he that teacheth man knowledge, shall not he know? (11) The Lord knoweth the thoughts of man, that they are vanity.

Psalms 141, Verse 3:

(3) Set a watch, O Lord, before my mouth; keep the door of my lips.

Proverbs 13, Verse 24:

(24) He that spareth his rod hateth his son; but he that loveth him chasteneth him betimes.

Ecclesiastes 10, Verse 2:

(2) A wise man's heart is at his right hand, but a fool's heart at his left.

Jesus, the Son of God: Isaiah 9 Verses 6-7

(6) For unto us a child is born, unto us a son is given: and the government shall be upon his shoulder: and his name will be called Wonderful, Counselor, The mighty God, The everlasting Father, The Prince of Pease. (7) Of the increase of his government and peace there shall be no end, upon the throne of David, and upon his kingdom, to order it, and to establish it with judgment and with justice from henceforth even for ever. The zeal of the Lord of hosts will perform this.

Whether your soul, lives or dies: Ezekiel 18, Verses 19-24 & 32

(19) Yet say ye, Why? doth not the son bear the iniquity of the father? When the son hath done that which is lawful and right, and hath kept all my statutes, and hath done them, he shall surely live. (20) The soul that sinneth it shall die. The son shall not bear the iniquity of the father, neither shall the father bear the iniquity of the son; the righteousness of the righteous shall be upon him, and the wickedness of the wicked shall be upon him. (21) But if the wicked will turn from all his sins that he hath committed, and keep all my statutes, and do that which

is lawful and right, he shall surely live, he shall not die. (22) All his transgressions that he hath committed, they shall not be mentioned unto him: in his righteousness that he hath done he shall live. (23) Have I any pleasure at all that the wicked, should die? Saith the Lord God: and not that he should return from his ways, and live? (24) But when the righteous turneth away from his righteousness, and committeth iniquity, and doeth according to all the abominations that the wicked man doeth, shall he live? All his righteousness that he hath done shall not be mentioned: in his trespass that he hath trespassed and in his sin that he hath sinned, in them shall he die. (32) For I have no pleasure in the death of him that dieth, saith the Lord God: wherefore turn yourselves, and live ye.

Daniel's Vision of God? And Jesus? Daniel 7, Verses 2-3 & 9-11 &13-15

(2) Daniel spake and said: I saw in my vision by night, and, behold, the four winds of the heaven strove upon the great sea. (3) And four great beasts came up from the sea, diverse one from another. (9) I beheld till the thrones were cast down and the Ancient of days did sit, whose garment was white as snow, and the hair on his head like the pure wool: his throne was like the fiery flame, and his wheels as burning fire. (10) A fiery stream issued and came forth from before him; thousand thousands ministered unto him, and ten thousand times ten thousand stood before him; the judgment was

set, and the books were opened. (13) I saw in the night visions, and behold, one like the Son of man came with the clouds of heaven, and came to the Ancient of Days, and they brought him near before him. (14) And there was given him dominion, and glory, and a kingdom, that all people, nations, and languages, should serve him: his dominion is an everlasting dominion, which shall not pass away, and his kingdom that which shall not be destroyed.

THE NEW TESTAMENT

Marriage: Matthew, Chapter 19, Verses 4–6

(4) And he answered and said unto them, Have ye not read that he which made them at the beginning made them male and female, (5) And said, For this cause shall a man leave father and mother, and shall cleave to his wife: and they twain shall be one flesh? (6) Wherefore they are no more twain, but one flesh. What therefore God hath joined together, let no man put asunder.

Marriage: Mark, Chapter 10, Verses 6–9

(6) But from the beginning of the creation, God made them male and female. (7) For this cause shall a man leave his father and mother, and cleave to his wife; (8) And they twain shall be one flesh: so then they are no more twain, but one flesh. (9) What therefore God hath joined together, let no man put asunder.

Divorce: Matthew, Chapter 19, Verse 3 and Verses 7–9

(3) The Pharisees also came unto him, tempting him, and saying unto him, Is it lawful for a man to put away his wife for every cause? (7) They say

unto him, Why did Moses then command to give a writing of divorcement, and to put her away? (8) He saith unto them, Moses because of the hardness of your hearts suffered you to put away your wives: but from the beginning it was not so. (9) And I say unto you. Whosoever shall put away his wife, except it be for fornication, and shall marry another committeth adultery. and whoso marrieth her which is put away doth commit adultery.

Divorce: Mark, Chapter 10, Verses 2–6 and 10–13

(2) And the Pharisees came to him, and asked him, Is it lawful for a man to put away his wife? tempting him. (3) And he answered and said unto them, What did Moses command you? (4) And they said, Moses suffered to write a bill of divorcement, and to put her away. (5) And Jesus answered and said unto them, For the hardness of your heart he wrote you this percept. (10) And in the house his disciples asked him again of the same matter. (11) And he saith unto them, Whosoever shall put away his wife, and marry another, committeth adultery against her; (12) And if a woman shall put away her husband, and be married to another, she committeth adultery.

"Jesus": Mark 10, Verse 45

(45) For even the Son of man came not to be ministered unto, but to minister, and to give his life a ransom for many.

"Jesus' Kingdom: Luke 1, Verses 31–33 (The Angel Gabriel speaking to the Virgin Mary)

> (31) And, behold, thou shalt conceive in thy womb, and bring forth a son, and shalt call his name JESUS. (32) He shall be great, and shall be called the Son of the Highest: and the Lord God shall give unto him the throne of his father David: (33) And he shall reign over the house of Jacob for ever; and of his kingdom there shall be no end.

Lord's Prayer: Matthew 6, Verses 9–13

> (9) After this manner therefore pray ye:
>
> Our Father which art in heaven, Hallowed be thy name.
>
> (10) Thy Kingdom come. Thy will be done in earth, as it is in heaven.
>
> (11) Give us this day our daily bread.
>
> (12) And forgive us our debts, as we forgive our debtors.
>
> (13) And lead us not into temptation, but deliver us from evil:
>
> For thine is the kingdom, and the power, and the glory, for ever.
>
> Amen.

The End of the Earth: Mark 13, Verses 24–27 and Verses 32 & 33

(24) But in those days, after that tribulation, the sun shall be darkened, and the moon shall not give her light. (25) And the stars of heaven shall fall, and the powers that are in heaven shall be shaken. (26) And then shall they see the Son of man coming in the clouds with great power and glory. (27) And then shall he send his angels, and shall gather together his elect from the four winds, from the uttermost part of the earth to the uttermost part of heaven. (32) But of that day and that hour knoweth no man, no, not the angels which are in heaven, neither the Son, but the Father. (33) Take ye heed, watch and pray: for ye know not when the time is.

The Twelve Disciples: Luke 6, Verses 14–16

(14) Simon, (whom he also named Peter,) and Andrew his brother, James and John, Philip, and Bartholomew, (15) Matthew and Thomas, James the son of Alphaeus, and Simon called Zelotes,(16) and Judas the brother of James, and Judas Iscariot, which also was the traitor.

The Twelve Disciples: Acts 1, Verses 13

(13) and when they were come in, they went up into an upper room, where abode both Peter and James, and John and Andrew, Philip and Thomas: Bartholomew, and Matthew, James the son of Alphaeus and Simon Zelotes, and Judas the brother of James.

Lawyers: Luke 11, Verses 46 and 52

(46) And he said, Woe unto you also, ye lawyers! for ye lade men with burdens grievous to be borne, and ye yourselves touch not the burdens with one of your fingers. (52) Woe unto you, lawyers! for ye have taken away the key of knowledge: ye entered not in yourselves, and them that were entering in ye hindered.

Death and Human Value: Luke 12, Verses 4–7

(4) And I say unto you my friends, Be not afraid of them that kill the body, and after that have no more that they can do. (5) But I will forewarn you whom ye shall fear: Fear him, which after he hath killed, hath power to cast into hell; yea, I say unto you, Fear him. (6) Are not five sparrows sold for two farthings, and not one of them is forgotten before God? (7) But even the very hairs of your head are all numbered. Fear not therefore: ye are of more value than many sparrows.

Forgivable Sins and Unforgivable Sins: Luke 12, Verses 8–10

(8) Also I say unto you, Whosoever shall confess me before men, him shall the Son of man also confess before the angels of God: (9) But he that denieth me before men shall be denied before the angels of God. (10) And whosoever shall speak a word against the Son of man, it shall be forgiven him: but unto him that blasphemeth against the Holy Ghost it shall not be forgiven.

Joy in Heaven: Luke 15, Verses 7 & 10

(7) I say unto you, that likewise joy shall be in heaven over one sinner that repenteth, more than over ninety and nine just persons, which need no repentance. (10) Likewise, I say unto you, there is joy in the presence of the angels of God over one sinner that repenteth.

How to enter Heaven: John 3, Verses 3–7

(3) Jesus answered and said unto him, Verily, verily, I say unto thee, Except a man be born again, he cannot see the kingdom of God. (4) Nicodemus saith unto him, How can a man be born when he is old? can he enter the second time into his mother's womb, and be born? (5) Jesus answered, Verily, Verily, I say unto thee, Except a man be born of water and of the Spirit, he cannot enter into the kingdom of God. (6) That which is born of the flesh is flesh, and that which is born of the spirit is spirit. (7) Marvel not that I say unto thee, Ye must be born again.

Who has ascended into Heaven: John 3, Verses 13–15

(13) And no man hath ascended up to heaven, but he that came down from heaven, even the Son of man which is in heaven. (14) And as Moses lifted up the serpent in the wilderness, even so must the Son of man be lifted up; (15) that whosoever believeth in him should not perish, but have eternal life.

Eternal Life: John 3, Verse 16 and Verse 36

(16) For God so loved the world, that he gave his only begotten Son, that whosoever believeth in him

should not perish, but have everlasting life. (36) He that believeth on the Son has everlasting life; and he that believeth not the Son shall not see life; but the wrath of God abideth on him.

Eternal Life: John 12, Verses 25 & 26

(25) He that loveth his life shall lose it: and he that hateth his life in this world shall keep it unto life eternal. (26) If any man serve me, let him follow me; and where I am, there shall also my servant be: if any man serve me, him will my Father honour.

Eternal Life: John 14, Verse 6

(6) Jesus saith unto him, I am the way, the truth, and the life; no man cometh unto the Father, but by me.

God is Spirit: John 4, Verse 24

(24) God is spirit; and they that worship him must worship him in spirit and in truth.

Judgment: John 5, Verses 22–30

(22) For the Father judgeth no man, but hath committed all judgment unto the Son: (23) that all man should honour the Son, even as they honor the Father. He that honoureth not the Son honouret not the Father which hath sent him. (24) Verily, verily, I say unto you, He that heareth my word, and believeth on him that sent me, hath everlasting life, and shall not come into condemnation; but is passed from death unto life. (25) Verily, verily, I say unto you, The hour is coming, and now is, when the

dead shall hear the voice of the Son of God: and they that hear shall live. (26) For as the Father hath life in himself, so hath he given to the Son to have life in himself; (27) and hath given him authority to execute judgment also, because he is the Son of man. (28) Marvel not at this; for the hour is coming, in the which all that are in the graves shall hear his voice. (29) And shall come forth; they that have done good, unto the resurrection of life; and they that have done evil, unto the resurrection of damnation. (30) I can of my own self do nothing; as I hear, I judge; and my judgment is just, because I seek not mine own will, but the will of the Father which hath sent me.

Communion: John 6, Verses 48–51, 53–58

(48) I am that bread of life. (49) Your fathers did eat manna in the wilderness, and are dead. (50) This is the bread which cometh down from heaven, that a man may eat thereof, and not die. (51) I am the living bread which came down from heaven; if any man eat of this bread, he shall live for ever; and the bread that I will give is my flesh, which I will give for the life of the world. (53) Then Jesus said unto them, verily, verily, I say unto you, Except ye eat the flesh of the Son of man and drink his blood, ye have no life in you; (54) Whoso eateth my flesh and drinketh my blood, hath eternal life, and I will raise him up at the last day. (55) For my flesh is meat indeed, and my blood is drink indeed. (56) He that eateth my flesh and drinketh my blood dwelleth in me, and

I in him. (57) As the living Father hath sent me, and I live by the Father, so he that eateth me, even he shall live by me. (58) This is that bread which came down from heaven; not as your fathers did eat manna, and are dead; he that eateth of this bread shall live for ever."

The Resurrection and the life: John 11, Verses 25–27

(25) Jesus said unto her, I am the resurrection, and the life: he that believeth in me, though he were dead, yet shall he live, (26) And whosoever liveth and believeth in me shall never die. Believest thou this? (27) She saith unto him, Yea, lord: I believe that thou art the Christ, the Son of God, which should come into the world.

Judgment and the Forgiveness of Sins: Acts 10, Verses 42-43

(Peter speaking about Jesus Christ)

(42) And he commanded us to preach unto the people, and to testify that it is he which was ordained of God to be the Judge of quick and the dead. (43) To him give all the prophets witness, that through his name whosoever believeth in him shall receive remission of sins.

Salvation for the Gentiles: Acts 13, Verses 47 & 48

(47) For so hath the Lord commanded us, saying, I have set thee to be a light of the Gentiles, that thou shouldest be for salvation unto the ends of the earth. (48) And when the Gentiles heard this, they

were glad, and glorified the word of the Lord; and as many as were ordained to eternal life believed.

Lesbians/Gays: Romans 1, Verses 22-32

(22) Professing themselves to be wise, they became fools, (23) And changed the glory of the uncorruptible God into an image made like to corruptible man, and to birds, and four footed beasts and creeping things. (24) Wherefore God also gave them up to uncleanness through the lusts of their own hearts, to dishonor their own bodies between themselves: (25) Who changed the truth of God into a lie, and worshiped and served the creature more than the Creator, who is blessed for ever. Amen. (26) For this cause God gave them up unto vile affections: for even their women did change the natural use into that which is against nature: (27) And likewise also the men, leaving the natural use of the woman, burned in their lust one toward another; men with men working that which is unseemly, and receiving in themselves that recompence of their error which was meet. (28) And even as they did not like to retain God in their knowledge, God gave them over to a reprobate mind, to do those things which are not convenient; (29) Being filled with all unrighteousness, fornication, wickedness, covetousness, maliciousness; full of envy, murder, debate, deceit, malignity, whisperers, (30) Backbiters, haters of God, despiteful, proud, boasters, inventors of evil things, disobedient to parents, (31) Without understanding, covenant breakers, without natural affec-

tion, implacable, unmerciful: (32) Who knowing the judgment of God that they which commit such things are worthy of death, not only do the same, but have pleasure in them that do them.

Value and purpose of Baptism: Romans 6, Verses 3-10, 12

(3) Know ye not, that so many of us as were baptized into Jesus Christ were baptized into his death? (4) Therefore we are buried with him by baptism into death: that like as Christ was raised up from the dead by the glory of the Father, even so we also should walk in newness of life. (5) For if we have been planted together in the likeness of his death, we shall be also in the likeness of his resurrection: (6) Knowing this, that our old man is crucified with him, that the body of sin might be destroyed, that henceforth we should not serve sin. (7) For he that is dead is freed from sin. (8) Now if we be dead with Christ, we believe that we shall also live with him: (9) Knowing that Christ being raised from the dead dieth no more; death hath no more dominion over him. (10) For in that he died, he died unto sin once: but in that he liveth, he liveth unto God. (12) Let not sin therefore reign in your mortal body, that ye should obey it in the lusts thereof.

Saved: Romans 10, Verses 9-13

(9) That if thou shalt confess with thy mouth the Lord Jesus, and shalt believe in thine heart that God hath raised him from the dead, thou shalt be saved. (10) For with the heart man believeth unto

righteousness; and with the mouth confession is made unto salvation. (11) For the scripture saith, Whosoever believeth on him shall not be ashamed. (12) For there is no difference between the Jew and Greek: for the same Lord over all is rich unto all that call upon him. (13) For whosoever shall call upon the name of the Lord shall be saved.

After Life–Heaven: 1 Corinthians 2, Verse 9

(9) But, as it is written, eye hath not seen, nor ear heard, neither have entered into the heart of man, the things which God hath prepared for them that love him.

The order of: God, Jesus Christ, Man & Woman: 1 Corinthians 11, Verses 3, 7-9, 11-13

(3) But I would have you know, that the head of every man is Christ; and the head of the woman is the man; and the head of Christ is God. (7) For a man indeed ought not to cover his head, forasmuch as he is the image and glory of God: but the woman is the glory of man. (8) For the man is not of the woman; but the woman of the man. (9) Neither was the man created for the woman; but the woman for the man. (11) Nevertheless, neither is the man without the woman, neither the woman without the man, in the Lord. (12) For as the woman is of the man, even so is the man also by the woman; but all things of God.

The Lord's Supper: 1 Corinthians 11, Verses 23-26

(23) For I have received of the Lord that which also I delivered unto you, That the Lord Jesus the same night

in which he was betrayed took bread: (24) And when he had given thanks, he brake it, and said, Take eat: this is my body, which is broken for you: this do in remembrance of me. (25) After the same manner also he took the cup, when he had supped, saying, This cup is the new testament in my blood: This do ye, as oft as ye drink it, in remembrance of me. (26) For as often as you eat this bread and drink this cup, ye do shew the Lord's death till he come.

Love: 1 Corinthians 13, Verses 4-13

> (4) Love is patient and kind; love is not jealous or boastful; (5) it is not arrogant or rude. Love does not insist on its own way; it is not irritable or resentful; (6) it does not rejoice at wrong, but rejoices in the right. (7) Love bears all things, believes all things, hopes all things, endures all things. (8) Love never ends; as for prophecies, they will pass away; as for tongues, they will cease; as for knowledge, it will pass away. (9) For our knowledge is imperfect and our prophecy is imperfect; (10) but when the perfect comes, the imperfect will pass away. (11) When I was child, I spoke like a child, I thought like a child, I reasoned like a child, when I became a man, I gave up childish ways. (12) For now we see in a mirror dimly, but then face to face. Now I know in part; then I shall understand fully, even as I have been fully understood. (13) So faith, hope, love abide, these three; but the greatest of these in love.

Women & Church: 1 Corinthians 14, Verses 34 & 35

(34) Let your women keep silence in the churches: for it is not permitted unto them to speak; but they are commanded to be under obedience, as also saith the law. (35) And if they will learn any thing, let them ask their husbands at home; for it is a shame for women to speak in the church.

The Resurrection: 1 Corinthians 15, Verses 20-26

(20) But now is Christ risen from the dead, and become the first fruits of them that slept. (21) For since by man came death, by man came also the resurrection of the dead. (22) For as in Adam all die, even so in Christ shall all be made alive. (23) But every man in his own order: Christ the first fruits; afterward they that are Christ's at his coming. (24) Then cometh the end, when he shall have delivered up the kingdom to God, even the Father; when he shall have put down all rule and all authority and power. (25) For he must reign til he hath put all his enemies under his feet. (26) The last enemy that shall be destroyed is death.

Judgment: 2 Corinthians 5, verse 10

(10) For we must all appear before the judgment seat of Christ; that every one may receive the things done in his body, according to that he hath done, whether it be good or bad.

Jesus' brother James: Galatians 1, verse 19

(19) But other of the apostles saw I none, save James the Lord's brother.

Gentiles saved: Galatians 3, verses 6-14

(6) Even as Abraham believed God, and it was accounted to him for righteousness. (7) Know ye therefore that they which are of faith, the same are the children of Abraham. (8) And the scripture, foreseeing that God would justify the heathen through faith, preached before the gospel unto Abraham, saying, In thee shall all nations be blessed. (9) So then they which be of faith are blessed with faithful Abraham. (10) For as many as are of the works of the law are under the curse: for it is written, Cursed is every one that continueth not in all things which are written in the book of the law to do them. (11) But that no man is justified by the law in the sight of God, it is evident: for, The just shall live by faith. (12) And the law is not of faith; but, The man that doeth them shall live in them. (13) Christ hath redeemed us from the curse of the law, being made a curse for us: for it is written, Cursed is every one that hanegth on a tree: (14) That the blessing of Abraham might come on the Gentiles through Jesus Christ; that we might receive the promise of the Spirit through faith.

Gentiles Saved: Ephesians 3, verses 1-6

(1) For this cause I, Paul, the prisoner of Jesus Christ for you Gentiles, (2) If ye have heard of the dispensation of the grace of God which is given me to youward: (3) How that by revelation he made known unto me the mystery; (as I wrote afore in few words, (4) Whereby, when ye read, ye may understand my knowledge in the mystery of Christ) (5) Which in

other ages was not made known unto the sons of men, as it is now revealed unto his holy apostles and prophets by the Spirit; (6) That the Gentiles should be fellow heirs, and of the same body, and partakers of his promise in Christ by the gospel:

Death through Baptism: Colossians 2, verse 12

(12) Buried with him in baptism, wherein also ye are risen with him through the faith of the operation of God, who hath raised him from the dead.

Forgiveness of Sins: Colossians 2, verses 13 & 14

(13) And you, being dead in your sins and the uncircumcision of your flesh, hath he quickened together with him, having forgiven you all trespasses; (14) Blotting out the handwriting of ordinances that was against us, which was contrary to us, and took it out of the way, nailing it to the cross.

How we should live: Colossians 3, verses 1-25

(1) If ye then be risen with Christ, seek those things which are above, where Christ sitteth on the right hand of God. (2) Set your affection on things above, not on things on the earth. (3) For ye are dead, and your life is hid with Christ in God. (4) When Christ, who is our life, shall appear, then shall ye also appear with him in glory. (5) Mortify therefore your members which are upon the earth; fornication, uncleanness, inordinate affection, evil concupiscence, and covetousness, which is idolatry: (6) For which things' sake the wrath of God cometh on the children of

disobedience: (7) In the which ye also walked some time, when ye lived in them. (8) But now ye also put off all these: anger, wrath, malice, blasphemy, filthy communication out of your mouth. (9) Lie not one to another, seeing ye have put off the old man with his deeds. (10) And have put on the new man, which is renewed in knowledge after the image of him that created him: (11) Where there is neither Greek nor Jew, circumcision nor uncircumcision, Barbarian, Scythian, bond nor free: but Christ is all, and in all. (12) Put on therefore, as the elect of God, holy and beloved, bowels of mercies, kindness, humbleness of mind, meekness, longsuffering; (13) Forbearing one another, and forgiving one another, if any man have a quarrel against any: even as Christ forgave you, so also do ye. (14) And above all these things put on charity, which is the bond of perfectness. (15) And let the peace of God rule in your hearts, to the which also ye are called in one body: and be ye thankful. (16) Let the word of Christ dwell in you richly, in all wisdom; teaching and admonishing one another in psalms and hymns and in spiritual songs, singing with grace in your hearts to the Lord. (17) And whatsoever ye do in word or deed, do all in the name of the Lord Jesus, giving thanks to God and the Father by him. (18) Wives, submit yourselves unto your own husbands, as it is fit in the Lord. (19) Husbands, love your wives, and be not bitter against them. (20) Children, obey you parents in all things: for this is well pleasing unto the Lord. (21) Fathers, provoke not your children to anger, lest they be discouraged. (22) Servants, obey in all things your masters according to the flesh, not with eye service, as menpleasers; but in singleness of heart, fearing God. (23) And whatsoever ye do, do it heartily, as to the Lord, and not unto men; (24) Knowing that of the Lord ye shall receive the reward of the inheritance : for ye serve the Lord Christ. (25) But he that doeth wrong shall receive for the wrong which he hath done: and there is no respect of persons.

When Jesus Christ comes: 1 Thessalonians 4, verses 13-18 and 1 Thessalonians 5, verses 1-3

(13) But I would not have you to be ignorant, brethren, concerning them which are asleep, that ye sorrow not, even as others which have no hope. (14) For if we believe that Jesus died and rose again, even so, them also which sleep in Jesus will God bring with him. (15) For this we say unto you by the word of the Lord, that we which are alive and remain unto the coming of the Lord shall not prevent them which are asleep. (16) For the Lord himself shall descend from heaven with a shout, with the voice of the archangel, and with the trump of God: And the dead in Christ shall rise first: (17) Then we which are alive, and remain shall be caught up together with them in the clouds, to meet the Lord in the air; and so shall we ever be with the Lord. (18) Wherefore comfort one another with these words.

5 But of the times and the seasons, brethren, ye have no need that I write unto you. (2) For yourselves know perfectly that the day of the Lord so cometh

as a thief in the night. (3) For when they shall say, Peace and safety; then sudden destruction cometh upon them; as travail upon a woman with child; and they shall not escape.

The Purpose, The Reason: 1 Timothy 2, verses 1-6

(1) I exhort therefore, that, first of all, supplications, prayers, intercessions, and giving of thanks, be made for all men: (2) For kings, and for all that are in authority; that we may lead a quiet and peaceable life in all godliness and honesty. (3) For this is good and acceptable in the sight of God our Savior, (4) Who will have all men to be saved, and to come unto the knowledge of the truth. (5) For there is one God, and one mediator between God and men, the man Christ Jesus; (6) Who gave himself a ransom for all, to be testified in due time.

Money: 1 Timothy 6, verses 7-10

(7) For we brought nothing into this world, and it is certain we can carry nothing out. (8) And having food and raiment let us be therewith content. (9) But they that will be rich fall into temptation and a snare, into many foolish and hurtful lusts, which drown men in destruction and perdition. (10) For the love of money is the root of all evil: which while some coveted after, they have erred from the faith, and pierced themselves through with many sorrows.

The Evil Tongue: James 3, verses 6-10

(6) And the tongue is a fire, a world of iniquity: so is the tongue among our members, that it defileth

the whole body, and setteth on fire the course of nature; and it is set on fire of hell. (7) For every kind of beasts, and of birds, and of serpents, and of things in the sea, is tamed, and hath been tamed of mankind: (8) but the tongue can no man tame; it is an unruly evil, full of deadly poison. (9)Therewith bless we God, even the Father; and therewith curse we men, which are made after the similitude of God. (10) Out of the same mouth proceedeth blessing and cursing. My brethren, this things ought not so to be.

Do Not Judge Others: James 4, verses 11-13

(11) Speak not evil one of another, brethren. He that speaketh evil of his brother, and judgeth his brother, speaketh evil of the law, and judgeth the law; but if thou judge the law, thou are not a doer of the law, but a judge. (12) There is one lawgiver, who is able to save and to destroy: Who are thou that judgest another?

God's Mercy and Promise: 1 Peter 1, verses 3-9

(3) Blessed be the God and Father of our Lord Jesus Christ, which according to his abundant mercy hath begotten us again unto a lively hope by the resurrection of Jesus Christ from the dead. (4) To an inheritance incorruptible, and undefiled, and that fadeth not away, reserved in heaven for you, (5) Who are kept by the power of God through faith unto salvation ready to be revealed in the last time. (6) Wherein ye greatly rejoice, though now for a sea-

son, if need be, ye are in heaviness through manifold temptations: (7)That the trial of your faith, being much more precious than of gold that perisheth, though it be tried with fire, might be found unto praise and honour and glory at the appearing of Jesus Christ. (8) Whom having not seen, ye love; in whom, though now ye see him not, yet believing, ye rejoice with joy unspeakable and full of glory. (9) Receiving the end of your faith even the salvation of you souls.

Who is God: Revelation 1, verse 8

(8) I am Alpha and Omega, the beginning and the ending, saith the Lord,

which is, and which was, and which to come, the Almighty.

War in Heaven: Revelation 12, verses 7-12

(7) And there was war in heaven, Michael and his angels fought against the dragon; and the dragon fought and his angels, (8) And prevailed not: neither was their place found any more in heaven. (9) And the great dragon was cast out, that old serpent, called the Devil, and Satan, which deceiveth the whole world: he was cast out into the earth, and his angels were cast out with him. (10) And I heard a loud voice saying in heaven, Now is come salvation and strength, and the kingdom of our God, and the power of his Christ: for the accuser of our brethren is cast down, which accused them before our God day and night. (11) And they overcame him by the blood of the Lamb, and by the word of their testi-

mony; and they loved not their lives unto the death. (12) Therefore rejoice, ye heavens, and ye that dwell in them. Woe to the inhabiters of the earth and of the sea! for the devil is come down unto you having great wrath, because he knoweth that he hath but a short time.

The Devils Number: Revelation 13, verse 18

(18) Here is wisdom. Let him that hath understanding count the number of the beast: for it is the number of a man; and his number is Six hundred threescore and six.

Eternal Hell: Revelation 14, verses 9-12

(9) And the third angel followed them, saying with a loud voice, If any man worship the beast and his image, and receive his mark in his forehead or in his hand, (10) The same shall drink of the wine of the wrath of God, which is poured out without mixture into the cup of his indignation; and he shall be tormented with fire and brimstone in the presence of the holy angels, and in the presence of the Lamb; (11) And the smoke of their torment ascendeth up for ever and ever; and they have no rest day nor night, who worship the beast and his image, and whosoever receiveth the mark of his name.

The End of Satan/Devil: Revelation 20, verses 1-10

(1) And I saw an angel come down from heaven, having the key of the bottomless pit and a great chain in his hand. (2) And he laid hold on the dragon, that old serpent, which is the Devil, and

Satan, and bound him a thousand years, (3) and cast him into the bottomless pit, and shut him up, and set a seal upon him, that he should deceive the nations no more, till the thousand years should be fulfilled: and after that he must be loosed a little season. (4) And I saw thrones, and they sat upon them, and judgment was given unto them and I saw the souls of them that were beheaded for the witness of Jesus, and for the word of God, and which had not worshiped the beast, neither his image, neither had received his mark upon their foreheads, or in their hands; and they lived and reigned with Christ a thousand years. (5) But the rest of the dead lived not again until the thousand years were finished. This is the first resurrection. (6) Blessed and holy is he that hath part in the first resurrection; on such the second death hath no power, but they shall be priests of God and of Christ, and shall reign with him a thousand years. (7) And when the thousand years are expired, Satan shall be loosed out of his prison, (8) and shall go out to deceive the nations which are in the four quarters of the earth, Gog and Magog, to gather them together to battle: the number of whom is as the sand of the sea. (9) And they went up on the breadth of the earth, and compassed the camp of the saints about, and the beloved city: and fire came down from God out of heaven, and devoured them. (10) And the devil that deceived them was cast into the lake of fire and brimstone, where the beast and the false prophet are, and shall be tormented day and night for ever and ever.

Judgment/with the book of life: Revelation 20, verses 11-15

(11) And I saw a great white throne, and him that sat on it, from whose face the earth and heaven fled away; and there was found no place for them. (12) And I saw the dead, small and great, stand before God, and the books were opened; and another book was opened, which is the book of life: and the dead were judged out of those things which were written in the books, according to their works. (13) And the sea gave up the dead which were in it, and death and hell delivered up the dead which were in them: and they were judged every man according to their works. (14) And death and hell were cast into the lake of fire. This is the second death. (15) And whosoever was not found written in the book of life was cast into the lake of fire.

New Heaven and New Earth: Revelation 21, verses 1-8

And I saw a new heaven and a new earth: for the first heaven and the first earth were passed away; and there was no more sea. (2) And I John saw the holy city, new Jerusalem, coming down from God out of heaven, prepared as a bride adorned for her husband. (3) And I heard a great voice out of heaven saying, Behold, the tabernacle of God is with men, and he will dwell with them, and they shall be his people, and God himself shall be with them, and be their God, (4) And God shall wipe away all tears from their eyes; and there shall be no more death, neither sorrow, nor crying, neither shall there be any more pain: for the former things are passed away, (5) And he that sat upon the throne said, Behold, I make all things new. And he said unto me, Write: for these words are true and faithful. (6) And he said unto me, It is done. I am Alpha and Omega, the beginning and the end. I will give unto him that is athirst of the fountain of the water of life freely. (7) He that overcometh shall inherit all things; and I will be his God and he shall be my son. (8) But the fearful, and unbelieving, and the abominable, and murderers, and whoremongers, and sorcerers, and idolaters, and all liars, shall have their part in the lake which burneth with fire and brimstone; which is the second death.

God is Coming: Revelation 22, verses 12-13

(12) And, behold, I come quickly: and my reward is with me, to give every man according as his work shall be. (13) I am Alpha and Omega, the beginning and the end, the first and the last.

Changing the Bible/Gods Word: Revelation 22, verses 18-19

(18) For I testify unto every man that heareth the words of the prophecy of this book, If any man shall add unto these things, God shall add unto him the plagues that are written in this book: (19) And if any man shall take away from the words of this book of this prophecy, God shall take away his part out of the book of life, and out of the holy city, and from the things which are written in this book.

ADDITIONAL INFORMATION ABOUT THE BIBLE

The books of the Bible are organized in the order of topics versus when they were written. First are the books of law and then the books of the prophets.

The Bible was originally written in three different languages: Hebrew, Aramaic and Koine Greek.

There are sixty-six books in the protestant bible. There are seventy-three books in the Catholic Bible.

The Protestant Bible has thirty-nine books in the Old Testament and twenty-seven books in the New Testament.

The Catholic Bible has forty-six books in the Old Testament and twenty-seven books in the New Testament.

During the early 1600s fifty-four men worked on converting the books of the Bible which were written in Hebrew, Greek, and Latin to the English language. This would eventually become known as the King James Version.

The King James Version was printed in 1611 and had eighty books including the Apocrypha as a separate section.

In 1885 a new printing of the King James Version removed the books of the Apocrypha and also in 1901 when the American Standard Version was printed.

The Bible has been translated into 2,018 languages and is still the bestselling book in the world.

Some statistical numbers about the Bible

Books in the Bible: 66
Books in the Old Testament: 39
Books in the New Testament: 27
Shortest book in the Bible: 2 John
Longest book in the Bible: Psalms
Chapters in the Bible: 1189
Chapters in the Old Testament: 929
Chapters in the New Testament: 260
Middle chapter of the Bible: Psalm 117
Shortest chapter in the Bible: Psalm 117
Longest chapter in the Bible: Psalm 119
Verses in the Bible: 31,173
Verses in the Old Testament: 23,214
Verses in the New Testament: 7,959
Shortest verse in the Bible: John 11:35
Longest verse in the Bible: Esther 8:9
Words in the Bible: 773,692
Words in the Old Testament: 592,439
Words in the New Testament: 181,253

BOOK AUTHORS
OF THE BIBLE

Multiple Book Authors:	Author
Genesis; Exodus; Leviticus; Job; Numbers; Deuteronomy	Moses
Judges; Ruth; 1st Samuel	Samuel
1st Samuel; 2nd Samuel	Gad; Nathan
Song of Solomon; Ecclesiastes; Proverbs	Solomon
Lamentations; 1st Kings; 2nd Kings; Jeremiah	Jeremiah
1st Chronicles; 2nd Chronicles	Ezra
1st Thessalonians; 2nd Thessalonians; Galatians;	Paul
1st Corinthians; 2nd Corinthians; Romans; Ephesians	Paul
Colossians; Philemon Philippians; Hebrews;	Paul
1st Timothy; 2nd Timothy; Titus;	Paul
1st Peter; 2nd Peter	Peter
John; 1st John; 2nd John; 3rd John; Revelation	Apostle John
Luke; Acts	Luke

Single Book Authors:	Author
Joshua	Joshua
Jonah	Jonah

Joel...Joel
Amos ....Amos
Hosea..Hosea
Isaiah ....Isaiah
Micah ....Micah
Zephaniah ....Zephaniah
Nahum..Nahum
Habakkuk..Habakkuk
Obadiah.. Obadiah
Ezekiel... Ezekiel
Daniel.. Daniel
Haggal .... Haggal
Zechariah..Zechariah
Esther ....Mordecai
Psalms.. David
Nehemiah .... Nehemiah
Malachi..Malachi
Matthew .... Matthew
James ....James
Mark... Mark
Jude..Jude
Proverbs ....Agur; Lemuel

Who wrote the most books in the Old Testament?
Moses–six

Who wrote the most books in the New Testament?
Paul–fourteen (over half of the New Testament)

THE TWELVE DISCIPLES

Andrew

Bartholomew

James the Elder

James the Younger

John

Judas

Jude

Matthew

Peter

Philip

Simon

Thomas

How did the lives of the twelve disciples end? Eight disciples died as martyrs, James was put to death by Herod, Judas Iscariot committed suicide, and two disciples were crucified, Peter and Andrew.

DIFFERENT VERSIONS OF THE PROTESTANT BIBLE

King James Version... KJV
English Standard Version .... ESV
American Standard Version .... ASV
New Living Translation .... NLT
New International Version.. NIV
Young's Literal Translation .... YLT
Complete Jewish Bible.. CJB
Amplified Bible .... AMP
Revised Standard Version .... RSV
New Revised Standard Version.......................... NRSV

DIFFERENT VERSIONS OF THE CATHOLIC BIBLE

PROTESTANT BOOKS OF THE BIBLE

The Old Testament

Genesis
Exodus
Leviticus
Numbers
Deuteronomy
Joshua
Judges
Ruth
1 Samuel
2 Samuel
1 Kings
2 Kings
1 Chronicles
2 Chronicles
Ezra
Nehemiah
Esther
Job

Psalms
Proverbs
Ecclesiastes
Song of Solomon
Isaiah
Jeremiah
Lamentations
Ezekiel
Daniel
Hosea
Joel
Amos
Obadiah
Jonah
Micah
Nahum
Habakkuk
Zephaniah
Haggai

Zechariah
Malachi

The New Testament

Matthew
Mark
Luke
John
Acts
Romans
1 Corinthians
2 Corinthians
Galatians
Ephesians
Philippians
Colossians
1 Thessalonians
2 Thessalonians
1 Timothy
2 Timothy
Titus
Philemon
Hebrews
James
1 Peter
2 Peter
1 John
2 John
3 John
Jude
Revelation

CATHOLIC BOOKS OF THE BIBLE IN CANONICAL ORDER

The Old Testament

Genesis
Exodus
Leviticus
Numbers
Deuteronomy
Joshua
Judges
Ruth
1 Samuel
2 Samuel
1 Kings
2 Kings
1 Chronicles
2 Chronicles
Ezra
Nehemiah
Tobit
Judith
Esther
1 Maccabees
2 Maccabees
Job
Psalms
Proverbs
Ecclesiastes
Song of Songs
Wisdom
Sirach
Isaiah
Jeremiah
Lamentations
Baruch
Ezekiel
Daniel
Hosea
Joel

Amos	Hebrews
Obadiah	James
Jonah	1 Peter
Micah	2 Peter
Nahum	1 John
Habakkuk	2 John
Zephaniah	3 John
Haggai	Jude
Zechariah	Revelation
Malachi	

The New Testament

Matthew
Mark
Luke
John
Acts
Romans
1 Corinthians
2 Corinthians
Galatians
Ephesians
Philippians
Colossians
1 Thessalonians
2 Thessalonians
1 Timothy
2 Timothy
Titus
Philemon

DOES GOD EXIST?

Here are some reasons to say yes.

Scientific reasons to believe in design by a *superior* intellect so advanced that man cannot even begin to understand. What we think we know now:

The Earth:

The size is perfect. The earth's size and corresponding gravity holds a thin layer of mostly nitrogen and oxygen gases, which extend about fifty miles above the earth's surface. If the earth was smaller an atmosphere would be impossible (like Mercury). If the earth was larger, its atmosphere would contain free hydrogen (like Jupiter). Our planet earth is the only one equipped with the right gases in the atmosphere to sustain plant, animal, and human life.

The correct distance. The earth is located the right distance from the sun. The earth's temperature range is roughly -30 below to +120 degrees. If the earth were any further away from the sun, we would all freeze. If we were any closer,we would burn up. Even just a fractional variance in the earth's position to the sun would make life impossible.

The perfect rotation & angle. The earth rotates around the sun traveling at a speed of nearly 67,000 mph. It is also rotating on its axis so that the surface of the earth can be correctly warmed and cooled every day.

Precise yearly rotation. The earth starts at a specific point in its rotation around the sun. In exactly 365 days and six hours, the earth is exactly at the same point where it started from. A completed egg-shaped circle. When this continued rotation happens over a four year span.... we add one day to our calendar (6 hrs. X 4yrs. = 24 hrs. or 1 day). This generates what we call the Leap year!

The Moon:

Perfect size and distance. The moon is the perfect size and distance from the earth for it to generate its gravitational pull on the oceans. This creates ocean tides and movement so that the ocean waters do not become stagnate. This also aids in restraining the oceans from spilling over across all the continents.

Water:

Essential for life. It is colorless, odorless, tasteless, and made from the right combination of gases (hydrogen and oxygen). Plants, animals, and human beings consist mostly of water and could not survive without it. Water is chemically neutral. Without affecting the makeup of the substance it carries, water enables food, medicines and minerals to be absorbed and used by plants, animals, and human beings.

Two thirds of the earth is covered by water. The sun evaporates the ocean waters, leaving the salt, and forms clouds which are easily moved by the wind to spread the water over the land for vegetation, animals, and people. Excess water runs into rivers which in turn run back into the oceans. This continuous cycle of purification and supply sustains life on this planet.

Nature:

Uniform laws in place. Gravity remains consistent; the earth rotates on its axis the same every twenty-four hours; rotation of the moon; earth's rotation around the sun; the speed of light doesn't change—on earth or in galaxies far away. There are many different other laws of nature that we can identify that never change. Why is the universe so orderly and so reliable? The greatest scientists have been amazed at how strange this is. There is no logical reason why a universe obeys these rules, and why it abides by the rules of mathematics. Everything in the universe is mathematically sound.

God's SUPERIOR intellect:

Solar system protection. Jupiter is the solar system's vacuum cleaner, pulling in meteors and comets. Scientists estimate that if it was not for this amazing fact, the number of these objects hitting earth would be about ten thousand times greater.

*As the earth turns, the stars come back to the same place in the night sky every 23 hours, 56 minutes and 4.09 seconds. This is a sidereal day (star day).

*The earth actually takes 365.24219 days to orbit the Sun, which is called one Solar Year. To compensate for the missing 0.242 days, the western calendar adds an extra day in February every fourth (leap) year, but misses out three leap years every four centuries.

REFERENCES

Hunter, Margaret. "amazingbibletimeline.com." Accessed August 20, 2013.

United States Conference of Catholic Bishops, "usccb.org/bible/books." Accessed August 31, 2013.

Newbury Park, CA, "bibleinfo.com." Accessed August 31, 2013.

Scottsdale, AZ, "ministerBook.com." Accessed August 31, 2013.

Colorado Springs, CO, "gotquestions.org." Accessed August 20, 2013.

Adamson, Marilyn. "everystudent.com." Last modified March 03, 2009. Accessed May 17, 2012.

Rampur, Stephen. "buzzle.com/articles/books-of-the-bible." Accessed August 20, 2013.